Bond

UP TO *SPEED*
Verbal Reasoning
Tests and Papers

9–10 years

Frances Down

Nelson Thornes

Published in 2013 by:
Nelson Thornes Ltd
Delta Place
27 Bath Road
CHELTENHAM
GL53 7TH
United Kingdom

13 14 15 16 17 / 10 9 8 7 6 5 4 3 2 1

A catalogue record for this book is available from the British Library

ISBN 978 1 4085 1883 0

Page make-up by OKS Prepress, India

Printed in China by 1010 Printing International Ltd

Introduction

What is Bond?

The Bond *Up to Speed* series is a new addition to the Bond range of assessment papers, the number one series for the 11+, selective exams and general practice. Bond *Up to Speed* is carefully designed to support children who need less challenging activities than those in the regular age-appropriate Bond papers, in order to build up and improve their techniques and confidence.

How does this book work?

The book contains two distinct sets of papers, along with full answers and a Progress Chart.

- Focus tests, accompanied by advice and directions, are focused on particular (and age-appropriate) verbal reasoning question types encountered in the 11+ and other exams. The questions are deliberately set at a less challenging level than the standard *Assessment Papers*. Each Focus test is designed to help a child 'catch' their level in a particular question type, and then gently raise it through the course of the test and the subsequent Mixed papers.

- Mixed papers are longer tests containing a full range of verbal reasoning question types. These are designed to provide rigorous practice with less challenging questions, perhaps against the clock, in order to help children acquire and develop the necessary skills and techniques for 11+ success.

Full answers are provided for both types of test in the middle of the book.

How much time should the tests take?

The tests are for practice and to reinforce learning, and you may wish to test exam techniques and working to a set time limit. Using the Mixed papers, we would recommend that your child spends 45 minutes answering the 60 questions in each paper.

You can reduce the suggested time by 5 minutes to practise working at speed.

Using the Progress Chart

The Progress Chart can be used to track Focus test and Mixed paper results over time to monitor how well your child is doing and identify any repeated problems in tackling the different question types.

Always read this type of question carefully, as most will have similar <u>and</u> opposite options.

Underline the two words in each line that are most similar in type or meaning.

Example <u>dear</u>   pleasant   poor   extravagant   <u>expensive</u>

Take care with words, like 'dear', that have more than one meaning. Also watch out for similarly spelled words.

1	<u>right</u>	left	wrong	<u>correct</u>	delay ✓
2	<u>kind</u>	cruel	<u>sort</u>	brave	dirty ✓
3	shut	shout	<u>short</u>	<u>brief</u>	beef ✓
4	spear	sword	<u>dagger</u>	axe	<u>knife</u> ✓
5	<u>pull</u>	push	hall	<u>drag</u>	call ✓
6	year	<u>couple</u>	month	wife	<u>pair</u> ✓

6 **6**

Find a word that is similar in meaning to the word in capital letters and that rhymes with the second word.

Example CABLE   tyre   <u>WIRE</u>

Look at the word in capitals. Try to find a suitable similar word. Then experiment with rhyming words.

7	BREEZE	tinned	<u>wind</u> ✓
8	STRIKE	sit	<u>hit</u> ✓
9	COMPLAIN	grown	<u>moan</u> ✓
10	DASH	curry	<u>hurry</u> ✓
11	EXPENSE	lost	<u>cost</u>
12	LIFT	days	<u>RAISE</u>

6 **6**

Underline the two words, one from each group, that are the closest in meaning.

Example (race, shop, <u>start</u>)   (finish, <u>begin</u>, end)

Take one word from the left brackets and match it against the words in the right brackets. Repeat until you find a pair that are similar in meaning.

13 (hard, <u>simple</u>, close)   (extra, more, <u>easy</u>) ✓

14 (sweep, creep, <u>weep)</u>   (<u>cry</u>, laugh, run) ✓

15 (lots, <u>less</u>, none)   (<u>few</u>, many, complete) ✗

16 (stay, visit, <u>pile)</u>   (house, ignore, <u>heap)</u> ✓

17 (<u>stick</u>, branch, fruit)   (tree, <u>adhere</u>, eat) ✓

18 (mount, extend, <u>attempt)</u>   (<u>try</u>, chance, opportunity) ✓   ⑤ 6

Underline the pair of words most similar in meaning.

Example come, go   <u>roams, wanders</u>   fear, fare

			Look for the
19 hide, seek	look, search	calm, busy ✓	<u>most</u> similar pair.
20 hilly, flat	black, blue	<u>hint, clue</u> ✓	
21 entrance, exit	hare, hair	fury, rage ✓	
22 calm, rough	<u>fussy, particular</u>	stamp, tiptoe ✓	
23 ignorant, knowing	suppose, support	<u>alter, change</u> ✓	
24 <u>stack, pile</u>	store, stone	preserve, claim ✓	

⑥ 6

Underline the word in the brackets that is closest in meaning to the word in capitals.

Example UNHAPPY   (unkind   death   laughter   <u>sad</u>   friendly)

25 QUICK   (slow   <u>fast</u>   safe   needy   blue) ✓

26 STEAL   (roll   roam   rock   robe   <u>rob)</u> ✓

27 SUPERB   (ghastly   ghostly   grisly   <u>excellent</u>   entire) ✓

28 BLAST   (nuisance   energy   call   hole   <u>explosion)</u> ✓

29 REQUIRE   (<u>need</u>   poverty   relapse   relax   select) ✓

30 RULE   (pencil   straight   lever   <u>govern</u>   obey) ✓   ⑥ 6

Now go to the Progress Chart to record your score!   Total ㉘ 30

Find a word that is opposite in meaning to the word in capital letters and that rhymes with the second word.

Example   QUICK   grow   <u>SLOW</u>

> Look at the word in capitals. Try to find a suitable 'opposite' word. Then experiment with rhyming words.

1 COMMON   bear   _Rare_ ✓
2 WORK   vest   _RHST_
3 THIN   brick   _THICK._
4 FALSE   new   _True_ ✓
5 UP   noun   _DOWN_ ✓
6 WIN   news   _Lose_ ✓

④ 6

Underline the two words that are the odd ones out in the following group of words.

Example   black   <u>king</u>   purple   green   <u>house</u>

> Three of the words have something in common. Look for the link. In the example, it is colours.

7 eye   ear   trousers   <u>glass</u>   nose ✓
8 run   <u>whisper</u>   skip   jump   <u>think</u> ✓
9 apple   cabbage   <u>banana</u>   orange   <u>carrot</u> ✗
10 <u>even</u>   flat   <u>odd</u>   house   bungalow
11 chicken   <u>goose</u>   gerbil   rat   <u>duck</u> ✗
12 <u>sixteen</u> three   seven   nine   <u>fourteen</u> ✓

④ 6

Underline the two words, one from each group, that are the most opposite in meaning.

Example (dawn, <u>early</u>, wake)   (<u>late</u>, stop, sunrise)

Take one word from the left brackets and match it against the words in the right brackets. Repeat until you find a pair of opposites.

13   (welcome, <u>left</u>, go)   (beside, <u>come</u>, keep)

14   (<u>less</u>, alone, together)   (<u>more</u>, some, one)

15   (July, month, <u>winter</u>)   (day, autumn, <u>summer</u>)

16   (<u>dry</u>, mild, hot)   (humid, cloudy, <u>wet</u>)

17   (cake, <u>slack</u>, educate)   (taut, <u>taught</u>, torte)

18   (<u>dark</u>, lamp, moon)   (shade, night, <u>light</u>)

     6

Underline the pair of words most opposite in meaning.

Example   cup, mug   coffee, milk   <u>hot, cold</u>

Look for the <u>most</u> opposite pair.

19   lie, fib   frog, toad   <u>front, back</u>

20   fire, burn   hill, valley   <u>fruit, vegetable</u>

21   <u>pretty, ugly</u>   finger, thumb   gold, silver

22   <u>hit, miss</u>   stretch, extend   bring, buy

23   aged, old   lift, elevate   <u>start, finish</u>

24   exhaust, tire   expand, contract   climb, ascend

     6

Underline the word in the brackets that is most opposite in meaning to the word in capitals.

Example   WIDE   (broad   vague   long   <u>narrow</u>   motorway)

25   FULL   (complete   heavy   eaten   hungry   <u>empty</u>)

26   APPEAR   (<u>vanish</u>   see   seem   vanquish   send)

27   PROFIT   (money   <u>loss</u>   lose   loose   gain)

28   BREAK   (gap   meant   <u>mend</u>   sorry   sad)

29   LIGHTEN   (brighten   <u>darken</u>   fiery   flown   tighten)

30   DANGER   (warning   reckless   risky   peril   <u>safety</u>)

     6

Look at these groups of words.

A	B	C
Shapes	Royal titles	Clothes

Choose the correct group for each of the words below. Write in the letter.

1 shirt _C_   princess _B_ ✓
2 king _B_   queen _B_ ✓
3 triangle _A_   socks _C_ ✓
4 sweatshirt _C_   square _A_ ✓
5 prince _B_   rectangle _A_ ✓

(5) 5

Find and underline the two words that need to change places for each sentence to make sense.

Example She went to <u>letter</u> the <u>write</u>.

> *Read the sentence carefully and identify where it doesn't make sense.*

6 The <u>afternoon</u> fell steadily all <u>rain</u>. ✓
7 He ate his <u>fork</u> with a <u>sausage</u>. ✓
8 The current was <u>easily</u> but the fish swam <u>strong</u> upstream. ✓
9 It was a lovely <u>day</u> <u>sunny</u>. ✓
10 The waves <u>dragging</u> onto the beach <u>crashed</u> the raft ashore. ✓

(5) 5

Rearrange the muddled words in capital letters so that each sentence makes sense.

Example There are sixty SNODCES <u>seconds</u> in a UTMINE <u>minute</u>.

> *Use the sense of the sentence to help you. Be careful with spelling.*

11 The FRATFCI _Traffic_ lights changed to REGNE _Green_. ✓
12 Look SIDINE _Inside_ our new tent in the DNEGRA _Garden_. ✓
13 I draw straight NESLI _Lines_ with my RRELU _Ruler_. ✓
14 Our TIKENT _Kitten_ has grown into a big BYATB _Tabby_ cat. ✓
15 There are no PETMY _Empty_ TEASS _Seats_ on the bus. ✓

5

Fill in the crosswords so that all the given words are included. You have been given one letter as a clue in each crossword.

Use the given letter to place the first word.
Then place the other words one by one.

16

B	e	A	S	T
e		R		i
N	a	m	e	D
C		e		e
H	i	D	E	S

BENCH
BEAST
NAMED
ARMED ✓
HIDES
TIDES

17

G	a	t	E	S
		L		L
A	L	i	v	e
		O		E
T	W	i	S	T

TWIST
ALLOW
GATES
ELVES
ALIVE ✓

18

S	p	o	t	S
T		C		o
a	F	T	e	r
n		e		e
D	a	t	e	S

SORES
DATES
STAND
OCTET ✓
AFTER
SPOTS

19

S		S		S
P	a	N	i	C
i		e		o
C	R	e	e	P
R		r		e

SPICK
SCOPE
SNEER
CREEP
PANIC ✓

20

P	L	A	T	e
	a		a	
A	t	o	M	S
	e		e	
T	r	A	d	e

TRADE
LATER
PLATE
ATOMS
TAMED ✓

⑤ 5

Underline the two words in each line that are made from the same letters.

Example TAP   PET   <u>TEA</u>   POT   <u>EAT</u>

Scan the words quickly and see if a pair jumps out. If you don't see the answer, look through, word by word, at individual letters.

21	LAID	RAID	<u>RULE</u>	<u>LURE</u>	DARE ✓
22	BALE	<u>DEAL</u>	<u>DALE</u>	BLED	BALL
23	SHOW	WASH	<u>POSH</u>	SHIP	<u>SHOP</u> ✓
24	<u>PART</u>	TART	WART	PORT	<u>TRAP</u> ✓
25	MEAT	<u>MOTE</u>	<u>MOAT</u>	MUTE	<u>ATOM</u> ✓

⑤ 5

9

Rearrange the letters in capitals to make another word. The new word has something to do with the first two words or phrases.

Example spot   soil   SAINT   <u>STAIN</u>

First look at the clues. Then rearrange the letters to find the anagram.

26	jump	spring	PALE	_Leap_ ✓	
27	glass	sheet	NAPE	_pane_ ✓	
28	throb	sore	EACH	_ache_ ✓	
29	light	lantern	PALM	_Lamp_ ✓	
30	bitter	sharp	OURS	_sour_ ✓	

Complete the following sentences by selecting the most sensible word from each group of words given in the brackets. Underline the words selected.

Example The (children, boxes, foxes) carried the (houses, books, steps) home from the (greengrocer, library, factory).

> Work through the sentence, bracket by bracket, choosing the most appropriate word from each one.

1 If white (balloons, paint, snails) is added to (red, yellow, blue) paint, then you can make a shade of (pink, black, green) paint.

2 When I wake (down, up, on), I open my bedroom (door, carpet, curtains) and look out of my (leg, ceiling, window).

3 If (today, Monday, May) is Saturday, then tomorrow is (Wednesday, Thursday, Sunday) and yesterday was (Thursday, Friday, Saturday).

4 My brother is (baking, cutting, sewing) some (strings, cakes, weeds) and the smell is (dusty, untidy, delicious).

5 Polar (bears, moles, cats) live in the (jungle, Arctic, cupboard) and hunt seals for (drink, fun, food).

5

Choose the word or phrase that makes each sentence true.

Example A LIBRARY always has (posters, a carpet, books, DVDs, stairs).

> Think about what the word in capitals has to have.

6 A LAKE always has (waves, boats, water, fish, islands).

7 A JUNGLE always has (monkeys, plants, elephants, waterfalls, roads).

8 A PAIR OF BOOTS always has (laces, mud, an owner, soles, holes).

9 A COW always has (horns, milk, grass, hooves, calves).

10 A BOX always has (sides, a flap, a lining, a surprise, chocolates).

5

11

Underline the one word in brackets that will go equally well with both the pairs of words outside the brackets.

Example   rush, attack   cost, fee   (price, hasten, strike, <u>charge</u>, money)

> The answer might have two very different meanings. Check your answer goes with <u>both</u> pairs of words.

11 caring, generous   type, sort   (considerate, <u>kind</u>, nature, nurse, arrange)

12 extremity, end   empty out, pour   (<u>overbalance</u>, fall, tip, nib, edge)

13 attach, fasten   dead heat,   (tie, connect, link, equal, bolt)
                        same level

14 knock, rap   controls water,   (hot, cold, <u>tap</u>, strike, blow)
                        a pipe stop

15 pen, yard   hit, beat   (batter, <u>hammer</u>, money, crush, pound)

5

Underline two words, one from each group, that go together to form a new word. The word in the first group always comes first.

Example   (hand, <u>green</u>, for)   (light, <u>house</u>, sure)

> Take one word at a time from the left brackets and put it in front of each of the words in the right brackets.

16 (star, swim, <u>car</u>)   (pet, pull, pit)

17 (<u>sauce</u>, pot, spilt)   (twin, flour, <u>pan</u>)

18 (<u>pea</u>, bean, swede)   (net, <u>nut</u>, not)

19 (tire, car, <u>wheel</u>)   (some, there, <u>few</u>)

20 (<u>rot</u>, make, best)   (ten, nine, four)

5

Underline the one word in each group that **cannot be made** from the letters of the word in capital letters.

Example STATIONERY   stone   tyres   ration   <u>nation</u>   noisy

> Look for any letters that are not in the word in capitals and for repeats of letters.

21 BRAMBLE   lamb   barb   real   (pram)   male

22 COTTAGE   gate   (sage)   goat   teat   cage

23 PICTURE   pure   tire   epic   (care)   true

24 SPATULA   (trap)   laps   past   last   pals

25 KINGDOM   monk   mink   dong   mind   (dine)

(5)

Underline the one word in each group that **can be made** from the letters of the word in capital letters.

Example CHAMPION   camping   notch   peach   cramp   <u>chimp</u>

> This time, only one word can be made from the word in capitals. Look, particularly, at the vowels.

26 LETTUCE   (cute)   teal   feet   tuck   cell

27 EXCITED   site   dent   toxic   text   (dice)

28 JUGGLED   deal   lead   glad   jade   (glue)

29 PHANTOM   chat   (moat)   tone   then   shop

30 DAZZLED   jazz   sled   eddy   read   (zeal)

(5)

Which one letter can be added to the front of all of these words to make new words?

Example   __are   __at   __rate   __all   <u>c</u>

> Experiment with putting various letters in front of each of the words until you find the correct one.

1   __lasted   __reads   __link   __lender   *b*

2   *m*ending   __ode   __ate   __allow   *m*

3   __lope   __very   __merge   __at   *e*

4   __trapping   __tart   __welling   __witch   *s*

5   __our   __east   __ourselves   __ear   *y*

5

Find the letter that will end the first word and start the second word.

Example   drow (<u>n</u>) ought

6   crea (__) onkey

7   polic (__) ndless

8   part (__) oung

9   nigh (__) witch

10   spel (__) augh

> Look at the word on the left and find various letters that could finish that word. Then see which one you can also use to start the word on the right.

5

Find the letter that will complete both pairs of words, ending the first word and starting the second. The same letter must be used for both pairs of words.

Example   mea (<u>t</u>) able   fi (<u>t</u>) ub

11   walkin (__) reen   flun (__) lide

12   kick (__) wallow   bat (__) alt

13   niec (__) lder   budg (__) very

14   himsel (__) inger   hoo (__) aster

15   pa (__) illow   co (__) indow

5

Move one letter from the first word to the second word to make two new words.

Example   hunt   sip   <u>hut</u>   <u>snip</u>

> Take a letter at a time from the first word and see if you can make a separate word. Then see if you can put the letter into the second word to make a new word.

16 pipe   hum   _____   _____

17 pant   hit   _____   _____

18 clap   art   _____   _____

19 bite   not   _____   _____

20 home   end   _____   _____   **5**

Add one letter to the word in capital letters to make a new word. The meaning of the new word is given in the clue.

> Add suitable letters to the word in capitals and think about the meaning to help you. Alternatively, you could look at the meaning and find a word that uses the letters given on the left.

Example   PLAN   simple   <u>PLAIN</u>

21 BOTH   soup   _____

22 NICE   relation   _____

23 PACE   calm   _____

24 LUCK   fortunate   _____

25 SAME   disgrace   _____   **5**

Remove one letter from the word in capital letters to leave a new word. The meaning of the new word is given in the clue.

Example   AUNT   an insect   <u>ANT</u>

26 CLAPS   hats   _____

27 SIGHT   breathe out   _____

28 STEAM   stalk   _____

29 BEAST   finest   _____

30 FLAIR   den   _____   **5**

Change one word so that the sentence makes sense. Underline the word you are taking out and write your new word on the line.

Example   I waited in line to buy a <u>book</u> to see the film.   <u>ticket</u>

1 Giraffes have short necks to reach leaves in high trees.   _____

2 My ice pebble dribbled down the cone.   _____

3 George blew the presents out on his birthday cake as
   we sang 'Happy Birthday'.   _____

4 The sun shone and clouds blew across the green sky.   _____   **4**

Find the three-letter word that can be added to the letters in capitals to make a new word. The new word will complete the sentence sensibly. Write the three-letter word.

Example   The cat sprang onto the MO.   <u>USE</u>

5 I carried the supermarket BET for my mother.   _____

6 Archie has entered the school singing COMITION.   _____

7 We watched the RHORSES gallop fast up the racetrack.   _____

8 My aunt always brings a bag of SBET lemons when
   she visits.   _____

9 On URDAY, we are going to have a barbecue   _____   **5**

Find a word that can be put in front of each of the following words to make new, compound words.

Example cast   fall   ward   pour   <u>down</u>

> Look for common words such as up/down, hand/foot, and so on.

10 stage   shore   ward   line   _____

11 fly   cup   nut   fingers   _____

12 gammon   ground   pack   bone   _____

13 shine   light   day   bathe   _____   **4**

16

Change the first word of the third pair in the same way as the other pairs to give a new word.

Example bind, hind bare, hare but, <u>hut</u>

> See how the letters have been changed and continue the pattern. Take care with letter order.

14 feel, eel claw, law pray, _____

15 nut, net but, bet gut, _____

16 fan, wan fool, wool find, _____

17 damp, dam herd, her then, _____ **4**

Write the four-letter word hidden at the end of one word and the beginning of the next word in each sentence. The order of the letters may not be changed.

Example We had bat<u>s and</u> balls. <u>sand</u>

> Work carefully through the sentence, word by word. Sound out the possibilities.

18 The sugary water trap caught loads of insects. _____

19 Please attend carefully to what I am saying. _____

20 Snow fell overnight and covered the street. _____

21 My computer makes a funny noise starting up. _____

22 The road home was blocked by an overturned bus. _____ **5**

Look at the first group of three words. The word in the middle has been made from the two other words. Complete the second group of three words in the same way, making a new word in the middle of the group.

Example PAIN INTO T<u>OO</u>K ALSO <u>SOON</u> ONLY

> Letter by letter, see where the middle word gets its letters from. Repeat the pattern for the second group of words.

23 CALM CART FORT HUNG _____ LIMP

24 POOL PEEL MEET BARK _____ FOOL

25 JEST JAMS RAMS BILL _____ DONE

26 MESH RUSH TRUE PICK _____ CLUE **4**

Change the first word into the last word by changing one letter at a time and making a new, different word in the middle.

Example CASE _CASH_ LASH

> Write down the letters that remain the same. Substitute the remaining letters one at a time.

27 COOL   _____   HOOK

28 MADE   _____   TALE

29 FORK   _____   FOND

30 BEAT   _____   COAT

4

Read the first two statements and then underline the one option that must be true.

> Look for the statement that <u>has</u> to be true, using only the information you have been given.

1 Letters contain information. Letters are put into envelopes before posting.

   A Envelopes may have important letters in them.

   B Our postal service is good.

   C Birthday cards come in the post.

   D All letters have white envelopes.

2 All dogs should have collars. Some collars are made of leather.

   A All dogs have red collars.

   B A dog I know has a cloth collar.

   C A cat could have a collar.

   D A dog could have a leather collar.

3 A square has four equal sides. Squares are a type of shape.

   A All shapes have four equal sides.

   B A rectangle is like a square.

   C Some shapes have four sides.

   D A triangle has three sides.

3

Four friends, 1, 2, 3 and 4, like different foods. Friends 1 and 2 like pasta. The other two prefer rice. Friends 1 and 4 like sausages and chips. Friends 2 and 3 prefer curry. All of them like chicken except 1.

> Before you answer the questions, write down the foods and which child likes what.

4 Which is the most popular food?   _____

5 Who likes pasta as well as chicken?   _____

6 Who likes curry and rice, but not sausages and chips?   _____

3

Eli's house is opposite mine. Mine is number 27. I live on the odd side of the road, he lives on the even side. There are forty houses altogether. If number 1 is opposite number 2 and 3 is opposite 4 and so on, answer these questions.

> Before you start, work out the pattern on a piece of paper.

7 Which house is opposite number 8? _____

8 What is Eli's house number? _____

9 One of Eli's next-door neighbours lives at number 26.
What number is his other next-door neighbour? _____

10 One of my next-door neighbours lives at number 25.
What number is my other next-door neighbour? _____

11 Asif lives in the house opposite number 37.
What number house does he live in? _____ **5**

Ananya has six felt pens that she keeps in a case. Below is a diagram of it. From the information, work out the order in which she keeps her pens.

1	2	3	4	5	6
			YELLOW		

The blue pen is between the red and green pen. The purple pen is not next to the yellow pen, neither is the green pen next to the yellow. The red pen is two places away from the orange pen. In which place number is each of the colour pens?

> Write a list of the pen colours and their possible positions.
> Eliminate the positions as you read through the information.

12 blue _____   **13** red _____   **14** green _____

15 purple _____   **16** orange _____   **5**

Here is a train timetable.

BILSTON (depart)	09:00	10:00	11:00	12:00
WAVENEY (arrive)	09:45	10:45	11:45	12:45

17 How long does the journey take from Bilston to Waveney? _____

18 If the 10:00 train arrived 15 minutes late, what time would I arrive at Waveney? _____

19 If I have an appointment in Waveney at midday, which train should I catch from Bilston? _____ **3**

Using the map on the right, underline the correct compass points in the questions.

20 Town A is to the (west, north, east) of Town D.

21 Town C is to the (east, west, south) of Town B.

22 To travel from Town C to Town A, you must travel first (west, north, east) and then north.

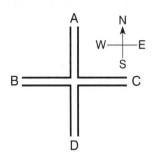

◯ 3

Maya is six years younger than Charlie, who is nine years older than Kyle, who is 8. How old is:

23 Charlie? ＿＿

24 Maya? ＿＿

◯ 2

If yesterday was Monday, answer these questions.

25 Which day of the week was it a week ago from today? ＿＿＿＿＿＿＿

26 What is the day after tomorrow? ＿＿＿＿＿＿＿

27 What is the day two days ago from today? ＿＿＿＿＿＿＿

◯ 3

Jason has £20 more savings than Kirsten, who has £17 less savings than Kieran, who has £34 savings. How much does each person have?

28 Kirsten ＿＿

29 Jason ＿＿

30 If Caitlin was 8 when her cousin, Tina, was born and she is 13 now, how old is Tina? ＿＿＿

◯ 3

Substitution and alphabetical order

If a = 4, b = 5, c = 3 and d = 2, find the value of the following calculations.

1 a + b + c = _____

2 c × b = _____

3 (d + b) − c = _____

4 a ÷ d = _____

5 (c + d) − a = _____

6 3b − (a ÷ d) = _____

> Replace the letters with numbers and work out the calculations.

6

If b = 1, r = 2, e = 3, a = 4 and d = 5, what are the totals of these words?

7 read _____

8 bear _____

9 babe _____

10 dear _____

11 bead _____

12 deed _____

> Add each of the letter values together to make a word total.

6

If the letters in the following words are arranged in alphabetical order, which letter comes in the middle?

13 CRIME _____

14 BARGE _____

15 DWELT _____

16 MINUS _____

17 SPORT _____

18 FOXED _____

> Write the letters of each word in alphabetical order, then pick out the middle one.

6

LEMON   APPLE   ORANGE   BANANA   PEACH

If these fruits are put into alphabetical order, which comes:

19 first? _____

20 third? _____

21 last? _____

SPELL   RAMPS   REALM   POSTS   SNAKE

If these words are put into alphabetical order, which comes:

22 second? _____

23 fourth? _____

24 last? _____

MERRY   MAGIC   MUMPS   MILKY   MOONS

If these words are put into alphabetical order, which comes:

25 second? _____

26 fourth? _____

27 fifth? _____

If the days of the week are put into alphabetical order, which comes:

28 first? _____

29 after Saturday? _____

30 after Tuesday? _____

12

Focus test 9 Codes

The code for FLOWER is 9 5 0 3 1 4. Encode each of these words using the same code.

> First line up the code with the word.
> F L O W E R
> 9 5 0 3 1 4
> Then substitute the letters for numbers.

1 FLOW _____

2 WERE _____

Decode these words using the same code as above.

3 9 1 1 5 _____

4 3 0 5 9 _____

The code for FATHER is % ? > < * +. Encode each of these words using the same code.

5 FATE _____

6 AREA _____

Decode these words using the same code as above.

7 > + * * _____

8 < ? > * _____

The code for EATING is h v f s w p. Encode each of these words using the same code.

9 NEAT _____

10 GNAT _____

> Make sure you write the code letters in lower case, not capitals.

Decode these words using the same code as above.

11 p v f h _____

12 p v s w _____

These words have been written in code, but the codes are not written under the right words. Match the right code to each word given below.

SOUP	POOL	LOOP	POUR
Y N D V	X N D Y	Y N N Z	Z N N Y

13 Y N N Z _____

14 X N D Y _____

15 Y N D V _____

16 Z N N Y _____

> Look for letters that stand out. Here, two words begin with P and one has a double O.

17 Using the same code, encode PLUS. _____ ◯ 5

18 If the code for FABLE is H T O W X, encode FEEL. _____

19 Using the same code as for FABLE, decode O T W X. _____

20 If the code for DIRTY is 7 3 5 1 8, encode TIDY. _____

21 Using the same code as for DIRTY, decode 1 5 8. _____

22 If the code for BRAIN is = + / # !, encode BARN. _____

23 Using the same code as for BRAIN, decode = / + =. _____

24 If the code for CRANE is s p m v z, encode CARE. _____

25 Using the same code as for CRANE, decode v z m p. _____ ◯ 8

The code for SPREADING is * Q 2 3 z U 4 > k. Encode each of these words using the same code.

26 SEED _____

27 IDEA _____

> Take care with writing the codes correctly.

Decode these words using the same code as above.

28 2 z 4 > _____

29 Q z k 3 _____

30 Q 3 z 2 _____ ◯ 5

Focus test 10   Sequences

Complete the following sentences in the best way by choosing one word from each set of brackets.

Example   Tall is to (tree, <u>short</u>, colour) as narrow is to (thin, white, <u>wide</u>).

> Find the relationship between the pairs of statements. The second pairing must be completed in the same way as the first pairing.

1 Hard is to (soft, difficult, wood) as wet is to (dry, water, droplet).

2 Fish is to (hook, scales, swim) as bird is to (goose, fly, sky).

3 Reply is to (touch, answer, write) as silly is to (sensible, foolish, responsible).

4 Impossible is to (possible, easy, fair) as impolite is to (rude, polite, quiet).

5 See is to (foot, saw, eye) as hear is to (there, ear, sound).

6 Rich is to (poor, money, strong) as take is to (tack, give, steal).

6

Fill in the missing letters. The alphabet has been written out to help you.

A B C D E F G H I J K L M N O P Q R S T U V W X Y Z

Example   AB is to CD as PQ is to <u>RS</u>.

> Look for the pattern in these sequences. Try putting your finger on the alphabet line and counting the number of spaces.

7 EF is to GH as UV is to ____.

8 TS is to RQ as PO is to ____.

9 DF is to HJ as LN is to ____.

10 OP is to QR as ST is to ____.

11 GG is to HH as II is to ____.

12 IH is to GF as is ED to ____.

6

Focus test 1

1 right — correct
2 kind — sort
3 short — brief
4 dagger — knife
5 pull — drag
6 couple — pair
7 WIND
8 HIT
9 MOAN
10 HURRY
11 COST
12 RAISE
13 simple — easy
14 weep — cry
15 lots — many
16 pile — heap
17 stick — adhere
18 attempt — try
19 look, search
20 hint, clue
21 fury, rage
22 fussy, particular
23 alter, change
24 stack, pile
25 fast
26 rob
27 excellent
28 explosion
29 need
30 govern

Focus test 2

1 RARE
2 REST
3 THICK
4 TRUE
5 DOWN
6 LOSE
7 trousers — glass
8 whisper — think
9 cabbage — carrot
10 even — odd
11 gerbil — rat
12 sixteen — fourteen
13 go — come
14 less — more
15 winter — summer
16 dry — wet
17 slack — taut
18 dark — light
19 front, back
20 hill, valley
21 pretty, ugly
22 hit, miss
23 start, finish
24 expand, contract
25 empty

Focus test 3

1 shirt C; princess B
2 king B; queen B
3 triangle A; socks C
4 sweatshirt C; square A
5 prince B; rectangle A
6 <u>afternoon</u> <u>rain</u>
7 <u>fork</u> <u>sausage</u>
8 <u>easily</u> <u>strong</u>
9 <u>day</u> <u>sunny</u>
10 <u>dragging</u> <u>crashed</u>
11 traffic — green
12 inside — garden
13 lines — ruler
14 kitten — tabby
15 empty — seats

16

17

18

19

S		S		S
P	A	N	I	C
I		E		O
C	R	E	E	P
K		R		E

20

P	L	A	T	E
	A		A	
A	T	O	M	S
	E		E	
T	R	A	D	E

21 RULE — LURE
22 DEAL — DALE
23 POSH — SHOP
24 PART — TRAP
25 MOAT — ATOM
26 LEAP
27 PANE
28 ACHE
29 LAMP
30 SOUR

Focus test 4

1 paint red pink
2 up curtains window
3 today Sunday Friday
4 baking cakes delicious
5 bears Arctic food
6 water
7 plants
8 soles
9 hooves
10 sides
11 kind
12 tip
13 tie
14 tap
15 pound
16 carpet
17 saucepan
18 peanut
19 tiresome
20 rotten
21 pram
22 sage
23 care
24 trap
25 dine
26 cute
27 dice
28 glue
29 moat
30 zeal

Focus test 5

1 b
2 m
3 e
4 s
5 y
6 m
7 e
8 y
9 t
10 l
11 g
12 s
13 e
14 f
15 w
16 pie — hump
17 pat — hint
18 lap — cart
19 bit — note
20 hoe — mend
21 BROTH
22 NIECE
23 PEACE
24 LUCKY
25 SHAME
26 CAPS
27 SIGH
28 STEM
29 BEST
30 LAIR

Focus test 6

1 <u>short</u> long
2 <u>pebble</u> cream
3 <u>presents</u> candles
4 <u>green</u> blue
5 ASK
6 PET
7 ACE
8 HER
9 SAT
10 on
11 butter
12 back
13 sun
14 ray
15 get
16 wind
17 the
18 fins
19 seat
20 love
21 term
22 hero
23 HUMP
24 BOOK
25 BONE
26 LUCK
27 COOK
28 MALE
29 FORD
30 BOAT

ANSWERS

Bond UP TO SPEED Verbal Reasoning Tests and Papers 9–10 years

Focus test 7

1 A
2 D
3 C
4 chicken
5 2
6 3
7 7
8 28
9 30
10 29
11 38
12 2
13 3
14 1
15 6
16 5
17 45 minutes
18 11:00
19 11:00
20 north
21 east
22 west
23 17
24 11
25 Tuesday
26 Thursday
27 Sunday
28 £17
29 £37
30 5

Focus test 8

1 12
2 15
3 4
4 2
5 1
6 13
7 14
8 10
9 9
10 14
11 13
12 16
13 I
14 E
15 L
16 N
17 R
18 F
19 APPLE
20 LEMON
21 PEACH
22 RAMPS
23 SNAKE
24 SPELL
25 MERRY
26 MOONS
27 MUMPS
28 Friday
29 Sunday
30 Wednesday

Focus test 9

1 9 5 0 3
2 3 1 4 1
3 FEEL
4 WOLF
5 % ? > *
6 ? + * ?
7 TREE
8 HATE
9 w h v f
10 p w v f
11 GATE
12 GAIN
13 POOL
14 SOUP
15 POUR
16 LOOP
17 Y Z D X
18 H X X W
19 BALE
20 1 3 7 8
21 TRY
22 = / + !
23 BARB
24 s m p z
25 NEAR
26 * 3 3 U
27 4 U 3 z
28 RAIN
29 PAGE
30 PEAR

Focus test 10

1 soft   dry
2 swim   fly
3 answer   foolish
4 possible   polite
5 eye   ear
6 poor   give
7 WX
8 NM
9 PR
10 UV
11 JJ
12 CB
13 IJ   KL
14 RS   UV
15 QS   UW
16 JH   FD
17 DE   GF
18 YJ   ZK
19 VN   UL
20 CN   AJ
21 YZ   AB
22 XY   ZA
23 AZ   YX
24 12   6
25 30   10
26 60   50
27 24   28
28 G10   H12
29 9Y   7X
30 D5D   F9F

Mixed paper 1

1 circus   tickets
   evening
2 kittens   weeks
   playing
3 supermarkets
   fuel   food
4 noise   roadworks
   ache
5 birthday   cards
   parcels
6 APE
7 ATE
8 TEN
9 LIP
10 OWE
11 s
12 h
13 b
14 f
15 v
16 28
17 34
18 44
19 December
20 Stefan's
21 French A; yellow B
22 beech C; red B
23 purple B; black B
24 cherry C; oak C
25 Greek A; Spanish A
26 R
27 N
28 E
29 S
30 T
31 30   70
32 1   4
33 25   30
34 17   5
35 17   13
36 <u>fire</u>   ice
37 <u>box</u>   hole
38 <u>squash</u>   milk
39 <u>worse</u>   better
40 <u>puppies</u>   kittens
41 d
42 c
43 w
44 f
45 z
46 MIDDLE
47 HIDE
48 FATE
49 PIECE
50 TIRED
51 3 5 2 4
52 7 1 3 3
53 4 1 2 7
54 NUTS
55 SOOT
56 gear
57 pink
58 stag
59 toil
60 foal

Mixed paper 2

1 goat   pram
2 short   tree
3 start   begin
4 uncle   nephew
5 give   find
6 bend
7 soaked
8 mould
9 sore
10 story
11 fine
12 graze
13 tackle
14 spot
15 school
16

P	L	A	N	E
E		N		V
A	R	G	U	E
R		E		R
L	O	L	L	Y

17

C	R	A	Z	E
	A		E	
T	R	I	B	E
	E		R	
T	R	E	A	T

18

Q	U	E	E	N
U		X		E
I	M	A	G	E
T		C		D
E	N	T	R	Y

19

F		S		F
R	A	N	G	E
A		A		A
M	O	C	K	S
E		K		T

20

Q	U	I	C	K
	P		R	
A	S	H	E	S
	E		A	
S	T	U	M	P

21 raw — dear
22 pod — pine
23 net — stay
24 fin — draft
25 seam — stinks
26 13
27 11
28 14
29 13
30 10
31 Then
32 chin
33 sour
34 hand
35 term
36 ↑ ← ↗ →
37 ↓ → → ↑
38 ↑ → ← ↖
39 WEAR
40 NEED
41 BOLTON
42 DURHAM
43 LUTON
44 COULD
45 TOAST
46 light — noise
47 hand — foot
48 dense — skinny
49 aunt — father
50 cow — sheep
51 TOUR
52 THIN
53 EVIL
54 RASP
55 LOVE
56 plum
57 blackcurrant
58 grape
59 cherry
60 4

Mixed paper 3

1 6 2 0 1
2 1 0 9 4
3 4 1 0 6 2
4 NEAR
5 GREEN
6 CAR
7 LORRY
8 TRACTOR
9 JOKER
10 MIXED
11 D
12 C
13 A
14 £6
15 £17
16 tow — pull
17 rash — reckless
18 between — amongst
19 helping — assisting
20 caring — compassionate
21 easy — today
22 hard — ball
23 tea — cup
24 cake — large
25 You — I
26 CRAM
27 ITCH
28 HOSE
29 BEAK
30 REEK
31 FJ — FI
32 PO — NM
33 EV — FU
34 TO — YN
35 KL — MN
36 Nadia
37 Helen
38 Maisy
39 Gita
40 3
41 DIN
42 TEN
43 SUN
44 RAN
45 RAG
46 gems
47 wool
48 urge
49 faze
50 chop
51 FARM
52 JOKE
53 SOFT
54 CALM
55 POLE
56 strong, delicate
57 serious, foolish
58 life, death
59 under, over
60 sweet, sour

Mixed paper 4

1 BLOW
2 ANSWER
3 BORED
4 FOR
5 WISE
6 hinge — oiled
7 keys — drain
8 plays — piano
9 front — green
10 rough — bathe
11 SOUR
12 FALL
13 BOOT
14 NEAT
15 BOND
16 playroom
17 understand
18 jobless
19 managed
20 handsome
21 g p w d
22 w d w m
23 SHIN
24 VAIN
25 HISS
26 M
27 R
28 T
29 I
30 S
31 XY
32 RQ
33 MO
34 MN
35 TT
36 A
37 B
38 C
39 20
40 14
41 15
42 14
43 4
44 10
45 6
46 story — fable
47 hush — silence
48 spade — fork
49 hint — clue
50 icy — freezing
51 t
52 d
53 g
54 p
55 a
56 strain — stress
57 snap — break
58 find — discover
59 race — sprint
60 spell — charm

Mixed paper 5

1 PEARL
2 SQUID
3 BLACK
4 GRAIN
5 SLIME
6 STOP
7 MALE
8 TEAR
9 SLIP
10 DONE
11 5 6 4 2
12 1 6 3 4
13 5 6 8 2
14 5 2 2 8
15 FARM
16 3
17 6
18 1
19 4
20 2
21 inner — outer
22 evening — morning
23 dull — bright
24 useless — useful
25 common — rare
26 rue
27 stew
28 dear
29 fable
30 all
31 20
32 6
33 3
34 2
35 12
36 suitable, proper
37 stay, remain
38 still, motionless
39 discover, find
40 extend, enlarge
41 TALE — LATE
42 FELT — LEFT
43 RISE — SIRE
44 FLAIR — FRAIL
45 STALE — LEAST
46 roof
47 rails
48 Christmas
49 a football
50 eyes

51 m d f e
52 RAIN
53 2 3 4 9
54 HEED
55 MESH
56 ED   CB
57 EF   FG
58 ZA   BC
59 XW   VU
60 BC   DE

Mixed paper 6

1 FIRE
2 FLOW
3 REAP
4 STEER
5 SPARE
6 water
7 brain
8 after
9 wind
10 horse
11 16
12 10
13 9
14 20
15 19

16 11
17 12
18 10
19 13
20 10
21 bake
22 dead
23 teas
24 song
25 germ
26 bled   niece
27 grow   seals
28 bout   heard
29 tail   first
30 sail   snows
31 comfort, succour
32 path, track
33 snug, cosy
34 cool, unflappable
35 soak, drench
36 / D v h
37 N h 3 7
38 BASK
39 RAKE
40 FEAR
41 30   45
42 3   15
43 D10   C12

44 3Y   4X
45 4n   6p
46 RELAY
47 ROUND
48 RUNNY
49 Wednesday
50 Monday
51 dark
52 out
53 future
54 right
55 untie

56

57

58

59

60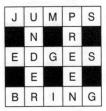

Give the next two pairs of letters in the following sequences. The alphabet has been written out to help you.

A B C D E F G H I J K L M N O P Q R S T U V W X Y Z

Example CQ   DP   EQ   FP   <u>GQ</u>   <u>HP</u>

13 AB   CD   EF   GH   ___   ___

14 FG   IJ   LM   OP   ___   ___

15 AC   EG   IK   MO   ___   ___

16 ZX   VT   RP   NL   ___   ___

17 DA   GB   DC   GD   ___   ___

18 UF   VG   WH   XI   ___   ___

19 ZV   YT   XR   WP   ___   ___

20 KN   IJ   GN   EJ   ___   ___

> Here, the letters in each pair are working separately.

◯ 8

Example RS   TU   VW   XY   <u>ZA</u>   <u>BC</u>

21 QR   ST   UV   WX   ___   ___

22 PQ   RS   TU   VW   ___   ___

23 IH   GF   ED   CB   ___   ___

> Treat the alphabet like a continuous line – XYZAB and BAZYX, and so on.

◯ 3

Give the missing two numbers and/or letters in the following sequences.

Example 2   4   6   8   <u>10</u>   <u>12</u>

24 16   14   ___   10   8   ___

25 ___   25   20   15   ___   5

26 ___   ___   40   30   20   10

27 16   20   ___   ___   32   36

> Look for the pattern between the numbers.

◯ 4

> In these questions, find the patterns for the numbers and the letters separately.

28 C2   D4   E6   F8   ___   ___

29 13A   11Z   ___   ___   5W   3V

30 C3C   ___   E7E   ___   G11G   H13H

◯ 3

Now go to the Progress Chart to record your score!   Total ◯ 30

27

Complete the following sentences by selecting the most sensible word from each group of words given in the brackets. Underline the words selected.

Example The (<u>children</u>, boxes, foxes) carried the (houses, <u>books</u>, steps) home from the (greengrocer, <u>library</u>, factory).

1 When the (circus, bus, rain) came to town last month, Dad bought (groceries, paper, tickets) and we all went one (evening, year, minute).

2 Our little cat had six (puppies, lambs, kittens) a few (weeks, seconds, minutes) ago and they are now (reading, barking, playing) as their eyes have opened and legs are stronger.

3 Big (cars, supermarkets, hotels) have pumps that sell (fuel, swimming pools, bicycles) as well as household things and (food, factories, fires).

4 The (noise, taste, smell) of the (roadworks, posters, lights) is making my head (dance, sing, ache).

5 On her (lap, chair, birthday) Amy received six (helpings, cards, berries) and two (rabbits, tissues, parcels) in the post.

5

Find the three-letter word that can be added to the letters in capitals to make a new word. The new word will complete the sentence sensibly. Write the three-letter word.

Example The cat sprang onto the MO. <u>USE</u>

6 I was given a new notepad with coloured PR for my birthday. _____

7 We will go for a run LR this afternoon. _____

8 Sonia's cat had three KITS. _____

9 Ice made the path dangerous and SPERY. _____

10 As it was so wet, our LAWNMR got stuck and would not cut. _____

5

Which one letter can be added to the front of all of these words to make new words?

Example	___are	___at	___rate	___all	<u>c</u>
11	___often	___ink	___inner	___elfish	___
12	___erring	___anger	___ours	___ate	___
13	___order	___lasting	___rainy	___lame	___
14	___lash	___alter	___lung	___right	___
15	___an	___omit	___alley	___ague	___

5

Stefan and Robert both support local football teams. Robert supports a team who play in a red strip. Stefan's team plays in blue. The boys kept a chart of the number of goals scored month by month. Using the chart, answer the questions below.

	October	November	December	January	February	March
RED	5	9	20	12	11	13
BLUE	7	11	9	14	17	13

16 How many goals were scored in February, altogether? _____

17 How many goals did Robert's team score in the first three months? _____

18 How many goals did Stefan's team score in the final three months? _____

19 In which month were the most goals scored? _____

20 Whose team, month on month, scored more goals? _____

5

Look at these groups of words.

	A	B	C
	Languages	Colours	Trees

Choose the correct group for each of the words below. Write in the letter.

21 French ___   yellow ___

22 beech ___   red ___

23 purple ___   black ___

24 cherry ___   oak ___

25 Greek ___   Spanish ___

5

If the letters in the following words are arranged in alphabetical order, which letter comes fourth?

26 HEART   ——

27 CANOE   ——

28 BRACE   ——

29 JUMPS   ——

30 FLUTE   ——

5

Give the missing two numbers in the following sequences.

Example	2	4	6	8	<u>10</u>	<u>12</u>
31	——	40	50	60	——	80
32	——	——	7	10	13	16
33	15	20	——	——	35	40
34	25	21	——	13	9	——
35	19	——	15	——	11	9

5

Change one word so that the sentence makes sense. Underline the word you are taking out and write your new word on the line.

Example   I waited in line to buy a <u>book</u> to see the film.   <u>ticket</u>

36 Ellie dropped a cube of fire into her drink to make it colder.   ————

37 The dog dug a box in the garden to bury her bone.   ————

38 Would you like squash and sugar in your cup of tea?   ————

39 Doctors treat sick people and make them worse.   ————

40 Olivia's tabby cat had five puppies last night!   ————

5

Find the letter that will end the first word and start the second word.

Example   drow (<u>n</u>) ought

41 pon (——) ishes

42 traffi (——) ount

43 pillo (——) indy

44 fluf (——) ather

45 buz (——) oo

5

Find a word that is similar in meaning to the word in capital letters and that rhymes with the second word.

Example CABLE   tyre   <u>WIRE</u>

46 CENTRE   fiddle   _____

47 CONCEAL   wide   _____

48 DESTINY   wait   _____

49 PART   fleece   _____

50 WEARY   hired   _____   ◯ 5

The code for BUTTONS is 4 2 7 7 1 5 3. Encode each of these words using the same code.

51 SNUB _____   **52** TOSS _____   **53** BOUT _____

Decode these words using the same code as above.

54 5 2 7 3 _____   **55** 3 1 1 7 _____   ◯ 5

Underline the one word in each group that **can be made** from the letters of the word in capital letters.

Example CHAMPION   camping   notch   peach   cramp   <u>chimp</u>

56 STRANGE   stun   gear   guns   tree   gain

57 PUMPKIN   pink   pack   inky   sunk   king

58 GHASTLY   cast   list   gale   stag   hate

59 PISTOLS   kiss   slow   plus   also   toil

60 FLAVOUR   rave   furs   love   foal   vale   ◯ 5

Underline the two words that are the odd ones out in the following group of words.

Example black   <u>king</u>   purple   green   <u>house</u>

1 kid   goat   youngster   child   pram

2 short   long   pine   yearn   tree

3 stop   start   halt   begin   finish

4 sister   aunt   uncle   nephew   grandmother

5 give   store   hoard   find   keep   ⟨5⟩

Underline the word in the brackets that is closest in meaning to the word in capitals.

Example UNHAPPY   (unkind   death   laughter   <u>sad</u>   friendly)

6 STOOP   (crawl   carry   tire   bend   fold)

7 WET   (soaked   rain   dry   desert   soften)

8 SHAPE   (square   mould   sign   rotten   solid)

9 PAINFUL   (sorry   sore   cry   grief   uneasy)

10 TALE   (story   moral   end   rhyme   poem)   ⟨5⟩

Underline the one word in brackets that will go equally well with both the pairs of words outside the brackets.

Example rush, attack   cost, fee   (price, hasten, strike, <u>charge</u>, money)

11 well, healthy   thin, light   (slim, skinny, fine, delicate, flimsy)

12 small cut, scrape eat grass,   (chew, slice, plaster, meal, graze)
                       snack

13 fishing kit,   face up to,   (rod, gear, tackle, angle, block)
    equipment   handle

14 notice, see   stain, mark   (spot, view, blotch, spill, perceive)

15 place of learning, coach,   (train, school, academy, college, tutor)
    education   instruct   ⟨5⟩

Fill in the crosswords so that all the given words are included. You have been given one letter as a clue in each crossword.

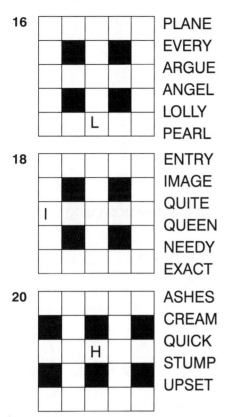

16

PLANE
EVERY
ARGUE
ANGEL
LOLLY
PEARL

(grid with L)

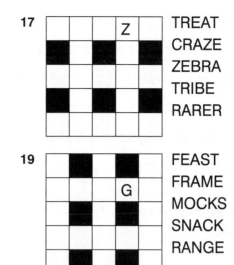

17

TREAT
CRAZE
ZEBRA
TRIBE
RARER

(grid with Z)

18

ENTRY
IMAGE
QUITE
QUEEN
NEEDY
EXACT

(grid with I)

19

FEAST
FRAME
MOCKS
SNACK
RANGE

(grid with G)

20

ASHES
CREAM
QUICK
STUMP
UPSET

(grid with H)

5

Move one letter from the first word to the second word to make two new words.

Example hunt   sip   <u>hut</u>   <u>snip</u>

21 draw   ear   _____   _____

22 pond   pie   _____   _____

23 neat   sty   _____   _____

24 find   raft   _____   _____

25 steam   sinks   _____   _____

5

If s = 1, t = 2, a = 3, l = 4 and e = 5, what are the totals of these words?

26 sale ____   27 teas ____

28 late ____   29 seal ____

30 last ____

5

Write the four-letter word hidden at the end of one word and the beginning of the next word in each sentence. The order of the letters may not be changed.

Example We had bats <u>and</u> balls.   <u>sand</u>

31 The noise from the aeroplanes was incredible.   _____

32 I looked at my watch in case we were late.   _____

33 That dog chases our cat whenever it can.   _____

34 In the park we played catch and some other games.   _____

35 I will master my fear of heights!   _____   5

The code for WANDER is ↓ ← ↖ ↑ → ↗. Encode each of these words using the same code.

36 DARE   _____   37 WEED   _____   38 DEAN   _____

Decode these words using the same code as above.

39 ↓ → ← ↗   _____   40 ↖ → → ↑   _____   5

LUTON   BOLTON   CRAWLEY   EXETER   DURHAM

If these towns are put into alphabetical order, which comes:

41 first?   _____   42 third?   _____   43 last?   _____

TRAIN   FRAME   CALLER   COULD   TOAST

If these words are put into alphabetical order, which comes:

44 second?   _____   45 fourth?   _____   5

Complete the following sentences in the best way by choosing one word from each set of brackets.

Example Tall is to (tree, <u>short</u>, colour) as narrow is to (thin, white, <u>wide</u>).

46 Heavy is to (light, difficult, wood) as silence is to (peace, noise, mark).

47 Arm is to (finger, body, hand) as leg is to (knee, sock, foot).

48 Thick is to (dense, slender, high) as thin is to (low, variety, skinny).

49 Uncle is to (aunt, brother, grandfather) as mother is to (baby, home, father).

50 Calf is to (field, cow, bull) as lamb is to (sheep, meat, fleece).   5

Rearrange the letters in capitals to make another word. The new word has something to do with the first two words or phrases.

Example	spot	soil	SAINT	<u>STAIN</u>
51	trip	outing	ROUT	_____
52	slim	skinny	HINT	_____
53	wicked	harmful	LIVE	_____
54	file	grate	SPAR	_____
55	adore	worship	VOLE	_____

5

Peaches, cherries and blackcurrants are round.
Grapes, plums and lemons are oval.
Peaches, cherries and plums have a single large stone.
The others have small pips.

56 Which fruit is oval with a large stone? _____

57 Which fruit is round with small pips? _____

58 Which fruit, besides a lemon, is oval with small pips? _____

59 Which fruit, besides a peach, is round with a large stone? _____

60 If a kiwi is oval with small pips, how many fruits, now, altogether have small pips? _____

5

Mixed paper 3

The code for DANGER is 6 0 9 4 2 1. Encode these words.

1 DEAR _____   **2** RANG _____   **3** GRADE _____

Decode these words using the same code as above.

4 9 2 0 1 _____   **5** 4 1 2 2 9 _____

5

    LORRY   CAR   VAN   TRACTOR   BUS

If these words are put into alphabetical order, which comes:

6 second? _____   **7** third? _____   **8** fourth? _____

    JOKER   MOUSE   MIXED   CRATE   JADED

If these words are put into alphabetical order, which comes:

9 third? _____   **10** fourth? _____

5

Read the first two statements and then underline the one option that must be true.

11 Mary is in Class 5. Class 5 is one of the classes at Willow Tree School.

    A Elise, Mary's friend, is also in Class 5.

    B Class 5 is next to Class 4.

    C Mary likes school.

    D Mary attends Willow Tree School.

12 Aidan and Ryan are twins. The twins have a baby sister, Freya.

    A Ryan is the older of the twins.

    B Aidan loves babies.

    C Freya has two big brothers.

    D Aidan and Ryan look after Freya.

13 Shaun has a new pair of school shoes. Shaun's school insists on pupils wearing black shoes.

    A Shaun's new school shoes are black.

    B Shaun's new school shoes are brown.

    C Shaun's shoes are a little bit tight.

    D Shaun walks to school in his new shoes.

    3

Callum has £11 more savings than Katya, who has £9 less savings than Joshua, who has £15 savings.

14 How much does Katya have?   ____

15 How much does Callum have?   ____

    2

Underline the two words in each line that are most similar in type or meaning.

Example <u>dear</u>   pleasant   poor   extravagant   <u>expensive</u>

16 toe   tow   leg   pull   push

17 sensible   rash   vibrant   reckless   alive

18 between   over   under   inside   amongst

19 helping   organise   correct   assisting   wrong

20 cruel   dirty   caring   simple   compassionate

    5

Find and underline the two words that need to change places for each sentence to make sense.

Example She went to <u>letter</u> the <u>write</u>.

21 The sums we did easy were today.

22 Ethan hit the hard ball and straight.

23 He drank his tea of cup slowly.

24 Mum cut four cake slices of large.

25 You wish I were in my class at school.

    5

Remove one letter from the word in capital letters to leave a new word. The meaning of the new word is given in the clue.

Example AUNT   an insect   <u>ANT</u>

26 CREAM   overfill   _____

27 WITCH   tickle   _____

28 HOUSE   pipe   _____

29 BREAK   bill   _____

30 CREEK   smell   _____   **5**

Give the next two pairs of letters in the following sequences. The alphabet has been written out to help you.

A B C D E F G H I J K L M N O P Q R S T U V W X Y Z

Example CQ   DP   EQ   FP   <u>GQ</u>   <u>HP</u>

31 FN   FM   FL   FK   ____   ____

32 XW   VU   TS   RQ   ____   ____

33 AZ   BY   CX   DW   ____   ____

34 TS   YR   TQ   YP   ____   ____

35 CD   EF   GH   IJ   ____   ____   **5**

Maisy and Gita have dark hair.
Nadia and Helen have fair hair.
Maisy and Helen have short hair.
Gita and Nadia have long hair.

36 Who has long fair hair?   _____

37 Who has short fair hair?   _____

38 Who has short dark hair?   _____

39 Who has long dark hair?   _____

40 Their friend Anna has long fair hair. How many now have long hair?   _____   **5**

Find the three-letter word that can be added to the letters in capitals to make a new word. The new word will complete the sentence sensibly. Write the three-letter word.

Example The cat sprang onto the MO.   <u>USE</u>

41 He was sent to change his T-shirt and wash his hands before NER.   _____

42 As the sun rose, the sky LIGHED and it became morning.   _____

43 Emily likes to BATHE on the beach in the summer.   _____

44 The ENTCE to the stadium was packed with people trying to get in.   _____

45 He parked the car carefully in the GAE and closed the doors.   _____   (5)

Underline the one word in each group that **cannot be made** from the letters of the word in capital letters.

Example STATIONERY   stone   tyres   ration   <u>nation</u>   noisy

46 GARDENS   gems   rang   dens   snag   near

47 PILLOWS   slip   wool   slop   slow   soil

48 TIGHTER   grit   rite   tier   urge   tire

49 FLAMES   same   slam   safe   fame   faze

50 BLOTCH   loch   both   clot   chop   bolt   (5)

Look at the first group of three words. The word in the middle has been made from the two other words. Complete the second group of three words in the same way, making a new word in the middle of the group.

Example PAIN   INTO   T<u>OO</u>K   ALSO   <u>SOON</u>   ONLY

51 JUST   JUMP   RAMP   FAIR   _____   WORM

52 LION   LIST   STEP   JOIN   _____   KEPT

53 HEMS   GUMS   GULF   RIFT   _____   SONG

54 BOAT   SOAK   SINK   HALF   _____   CRAM

55 BOWL   HOWL   EACH   MOLE   _____   DUMP   (5)

39

Underline the pair of words most opposite in meaning.

Example   cup, mug   coffee, milk   <u>hot, cold</u>

56 feeble, weak   strong, delicate   silver, gold

57 idiotic, stupid   serious, foolish   sensible, thinking

58 life, death   soon, presently   bind, bird

59 bizarre, strange   normal, ordinary   under, over

60 sweet, sour   drizzle, rain   made, maid

  5

Mixed paper 4

Find a word that is opposite in meaning to the word in capital letters and that rhymes with the second word.

Example QUICK   grow   <u>SLOW</u>

1 SUCK   foe   _____

2 QUESTION   dancer   _____

3 INTERESTED   afford   _____

4 AGAINST   paw   _____

5 FOOLISH   buys   _____   5

Rearrange the muddled words in capital letters so that each sentence makes sense.

Example There are sixty SNODCES <u>seconds</u> in a UTMINE <u>minute</u>.

6 The GNEHI _____ of my bedroom door needs to be LOIDE

_____ as it is really squeaky.

7 Poor Soolin accidentally dropped her SEYK _____ down a

RDANI _____ on the street.

8 She LAYSP _____ the IANPO _____ really tunefully
and well.

9 The NTRFO _____ door to our house is painted NGERE

_____ .

10 The sea was too GHROU _____ to THBAE _____ safely.   5

Change the first word into the last word by changing one letter at a time and making a new, different word in the middle.

Example CASE   <u>CASH</u>   LASH

11 SOUP   _____   TOUR

12 CALL   _____   FILL

13 BOAT   _____   BOOK

14 NEAR   _____   NEWT

15 BAND   _____   FOND   5

Underline two words, one from each group, that go together to form a new word. The word in the first group always comes first.

Example (hand, <u>green</u>, for)   (light, <u>house</u>, sure)

16 (play, walk, ring)   (toy, king, room)

17 (in, under, up)   (saw, stand, near)

18 (still, job, all)   (so, more, less)

19 (man, very, some)   (thin, aged, old)

20 (foot, hand, toe)   (full, some, dell)   ○ 5

The code for VANISH is g d b p w m. Encode each of these words using the same code.

21 VISA _____   22 SASH _____

Decode these words using the same code as above.

23 w m p b _____   24 g d p b _____

25 m p w w _____   ○ 5

If the letters in the following words are arranged in alphabetical order, which letter comes fourth?

26 SMILE ____

27 CRAZE ____

28 BUILT ____

29 FINCH ____

30 JUMPS ____   ○ 5

Fill in the missing letters. The alphabet has been written out to help you.

A B C D E F G H I J K L M N O P Q R S T U V W X Y Z

Example AB is to CD as PQ is to <u>RS</u>.

31 HI is to JK as VW is to ____.

32 PO is to NM as TS is to ____.

33 AC is to EG as IK is to ____.

34 WX is to YZ as KL is to ____.

35 ZZ is to XX as VV is to ____.   ○ 5

42

Read the first two statements and then underline the one option that must be true.

36 Betsy is a terrier. Terriers are a type of dog.

    A Betsy is a dog.

    B Betsy is a fierce dog.

    c Betsy has a blue collar.

    D Betsy goes for walks in the park.

37 Maidstone is a town in Kent. Kent is a county in the south-east of England.

    A Maidstone is an important town.

    B Maidstone is in the south-east of England.

    c There are many towns in Kent.

    D Kent is near London.

38 Daniel's school jumper is red. Daniel's school uniform is red and grey.

    A Daniel's school trousers have pockets.

    B Daniel likes his school uniform.

    c Daniel wears his red and grey uniform to school.

    D Daniel left his red jumper on the bus.

    3

39 If Zachary was 11 when his cousin, Grace, was born and she is 9 now, how old is Zachary? _____

40 If Jess was 7 when her cousin, Saul, was born and he is 7 now, how old is Jess? _____ **2**

If $u = 2$, $w = 5$, $y = 3$ and $z = 4$, find the value of the following calculations.

41 $w \times y =$ _____

42 $z + y + w + u =$ _____

43 $(y + w) \div u =$ _____

44 $(z \div u) \times w =$ _____

45 $(w + z) - y =$ _____ **5**

Underline the two words that are the odd ones out in the following group of words.

Example black <u>king</u> purple green <u>house</u>

46 story jest joke fable jape

47 rapid fast hush swift silence

48 diamond ruby sapphire spade fork

49 hint hind clue back rear

50 sizzling burning icy freezing fiery

○ **5**

Find the letter that will complete both pairs of words, ending the first word and starting the second. The same letter must be used for both pairs of words.

Example mea (<u>t</u>) able   fi (<u>t</u>) ub

51 min (__) able   stou (__) ear

52 rin (__) urable   swor (__) espair

53 flin (__) arage   bearin (__) one

54 jum (__) ear   shrim (__) arty

55 aren (__) zure   pizz (__) pple

○ **5**

Underline the two words, one from each group, that are the closest in meaning.

Example (race, shop, <u>start</u>)   (finish, <u>begin</u>, end)

56 (strain, freeze, bite)   (bounce, stress, melt)

57 (snap, crackle, pop)   (break, plod, mount)

58 (find, fine, fire)   (discover, lose, merge)

59 (choose, race, clear)   (cheer, sprint, claim)

60 (spell, bout, period)   (chart, chief, charm)

○ **5**

Mixed paper 5

Add one letter to the word in capital letters to make a new word. The meaning of the new word is given in the clue.

Example PLAN   simple   <u>PLAIN</u>

1 EARL   gem from an oyster   _____

2 QUID   sea animal   _____

3 BACK   dark colour   _____

4 GAIN   wheat, barley   _____

5 SLIM   mucus, goo   _____   5

Rearrange the letters in capitals to make another word. The new word has something to do with the first two words or phrases.

Example spot   soil   SAINT   <u>STAIN</u>

6 halt   stay   POTS   _____

7 man   boy   LAME   _____

8 hole   split   RATE   _____

9 slide   error   LIPS   _____

10 complete   finished   NODE   _____   5

These words have been written in code, but the codes are not written under the right words. Match the right code to each word given below.

FAME	HARM	FATE	FEET
1 6 3 4	5 2 2 8	5 6 8 2	5 6 4 2

11 FAME   _____

12 HARM   _____

13 FATE   _____

14 FEET   _____

15 Using the same code, encode 5 6 3 4.   _____   5

45

School lockers are in groups of six, as in the diagram.

LEFT	TOP	RIGHT
1	2	3
4	5 JUAN	6

BOTTOM

Will's locker was directly above Jack's. May's locker was not next to or right above Juan's. Fin's locker was on the bottom row below May's locker. Ali's locker was next to and to the right of May's locker.

From the information, work out which child has which number locker.

16 Will _____   **17** Jack _____

18 May _____   **19** Fin _____

20 Ali _____

Underline the two words, one from each group, that are the most opposite in meaning.

Example (dawn, <u>early</u>, wake)   (<u>late</u>, stop, sunrise)

21 (inner, middle, there)   (side, outer, centre)

22 (evening, noon, day)   (mourning, awning, morning)

23 (dull, thick, brassy)   (cloudy, gloomy, bright)

24 (useless, handy, bright)   (useful, worthless, pointless)

25 (common, under, extra)   (beneath, rare, more)

Change the first word of the third pair in the same way as the other pairs to give a new word.

Example bind, hind   bare, hare   but, <u>hut</u>

26 pair, air   pram, ram   true, _____

27 crab, crew   grab, grew   stab, _____

28 bean, dean   bell, dell   bear, _____

29 inch, finch   east, feast   able, _____

30 clowning, own   braiding, aid   stalling, _____

5

5

5

If m = 2, n = 5, p = 3 and q = 10, find the value of the following calculations.

31 m × q = _____

32 (p + n) − m = _____

33 (p + m + q) ÷ n = _____

34 (q ÷ m) − p = _____

35 (q − p) + n = _____

⬭ 5

Underline the pair of words most similar in meaning.

Example come, go   <u>roams, wanders</u>   fear, fare

36 idle, active   dream, wake   suitable, proper

37 fasten, release   stay, remain   into, onto

38 still, motionless   quiet, noise   never, sometimes

39 hide, seek   discover, find   appear, go

40 pretend, real   climb, descend   extend, enlarge

⬭ 5

Underline the two words in each line that are made from the same letters.

Example TAP   PET   <u>TEA</u>   POT   <u>EAT</u>

41 SEAS   TALE   SALE   LATE   TEAS

42 TELL   FELL   LEAF   FELT   LEFT

43 SURE   FURS   RISE   FIRS   SIRE

44 FLAIR   FRAIL   FAILS   SAILS   FAIRS

45 STALE   STALL   SEALS   LASTS   LEAST

⬭ 5

Choose the word or phrase that makes each sentence true.

Example A LIBRARY always has (posters, a carpet, <u>books</u>, DVDs, stairs).

46 A HOUSE always has a (garden, roof, person, flagpole, cat).

47 A TRAIN STATION always has (a road, a freight train, a guard, rails, four platforms).

48 DECEMBER always has (cold weather, Christmas, Mum's birthday, snow, floods).

49 A FOOTBALL MATCH always has (a football, grass, crowds, linesmen, a stadium).

50 A LAMB always has (white fleece, long tail, eyes, sheepdog, horns). ⬭ 5

51 If the code for BRAIN is m f d w e, encode BARN. _____

52 Using the same code as for BRAIN, decode f d w e. _____

53 If the code for HANDLE is 7 3 4 5 2 9, encode LANE. _____

54 Using the same code as for HANDLE, decode 7 9 9 5. _____

55 If the code for SHAME is ? & % £ +, decode £ + ? &. _____ ⬭ 5

Give the next two pairs of letters in the following sequences. The alphabet has been written out to help you.

A B C D E F G H I J K L M N O P Q R S T U V W X Y Z

Example	RS	TU	VW	XY	ZA	BC
56 ML	KJ	IH	GF	____	____
57 EB	FC	ED	FE	____	____
58 RS	TU	VW	XY	____	____
59 FE	DC	BA	ZY	____	____
60 TU	VW	XY	ZA	____	____

⬭ 5

Mixed paper 6

Rearrange the letters in capitals to make another word. The new word has something to do with the first two words or phrases.

Example spot   soil   SAINT   <u>STAIN</u>

1 burning   blaze   RIFE   _____

2 stream   pour   WOLF   _____

3 harvest   gather   PEAR   _____

4 drive   guide   TREES   _____

5 extra   pardon   SPEAR   _____   ◯ 5

Find a word that can be put in front of each of the following words to make new, compound words.

Example cast   fall   ward   pour   <u>down</u>

6 proof   tight   logged   melon   _____

7 wave   wash   storm   box   _____

8 noon   care   taste   thought   _____

9 swept   mill   surf   screen   _____

10 power   fly   back   shoe   _____   ◯ 5

In a changing room there are twenty pegs in two rows numbered 1 to 10 and 11 to 20. Number 1 is opposite number 11, 2 is opposite 12 and so on. Pegs 1 and 11 were already being used so I used peg 6 and Fiona used the peg opposite mine. Sophia used the peg at the end of my row and Jade used the peg next to hers.

11 Which peg did Fiona use?   _____

12 Which peg did Sophia use?   _____

13 Which peg did Jade use?   _____

14 What number was the peg opposite Sophia's? _____

15 What number was the peg opposite Jade's?   _____   ◯ 5

If f = 1, l = 2, o = 3, a = 4 and t = 5, what are the totals of these words?

16 loft ____   **17** flat ____   **18** foal ____

19 tool ____   **20** loaf ____

5

Underline the one word in each group that **cannot be made** from the letters of the word in capital letters.

Example	STATIONERY	stone	tyres	ration	<u>nation</u>	noisy
21	BACKING	king	gain	nick	bake	bank
22	DWINDLE	wind	lend	wide	line	dead
23	TRAINED	rind	teas	near	tide	dirt
24	PLEASING	ping	nail	pale	sign	song
25	FRAMING	gram	main	germ	firm	farm

5

Move one letter from the first word to the second word to make two new words.

Example	hunt	sip	<u>hut</u>	<u>snip</u>
26	bleed	nice		
27	grows	seal		
28	about	herd		
29	trail	fist		
30	snail	sows		

5

Underline the pair of words most similar in meaning.

Example	come, go	<u>roams, wanders</u>	fear, fare
31	keep, hide	comfort, succour	sit, stand
32	help, hinder	chew, swallow	path, track
33	snug, cosy	naked, clothed	quite, quiet
34	hot, icy	cloudy, windy	cool, unflappable
35	here, there	soak, drench	off, on

5

The code for BREAKFAST is N ^ h D v / D 3 7. Encode each of these words using the same code.

36 FAKE _____

37 BEST _____

Decode these words using the same code as above.

38 N D 3 v _____

39 ^ D v h _____

40 / h D ^ _____

〔5〕

Give the missing two numbers and/or letters in the following sequences.

Example	2	4	6	8	<u>10</u>	<u>12</u>
41	20	25	___	35	40	___
42	___	6	9	12	___	18
43	H2	G4	F6	E8	___	___
44	1A	2Z	___	___	5W	6V
45	3m	___	5o	___	7q	8r

〔5〕

RUNNY   RAPID   RELAY   ROUND   RISKY

If these words are put into alphabetical order, which comes:

46 second? _____

47 fourth? _____

48 fifth? _____

A B C D E F G H I J K L M N O P Q R S T U V W X Y Z

If the days of the week are put into alphabetical order, which comes:

49 last? _____

50 after Friday? _____

〔5〕

〔51〕

Underline the word in the brackets that is most opposite in meaning to the word in capitals.

Example WIDE (broad   vague   long   <u>narrow</u>   motorway)

51 LIGHT (pale   weight   dark   night   lamp)

52 IN (fashionable   clear   on   out   around)

53 PAST (gone   future   history   part   patch)

54 LEFT (dropped   missing   right   stay   play)

55 FASTEN (attach   tie   bind   secure   untie)

Fill in the crosswords so that all the given words are included. You have been given one letter as a clue in each crossword.

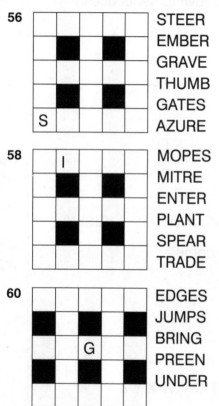

56   STEER
     EMBER
     GRAVE
     THUMB
     GATES
     AZURE

57   SNARL
     TRUST
     ROWAN
     SWEPT
     SUPER

58   MOPES
     MITRE
     ENTER
     PLANT
     SPEAR
     TRADE

59   ABOVE
     LASTS
     YEARN
     BLAME
     VOTER

60   EDGES
     JUMPS
     BRING
     PREEN
     UNDER